EOIN McANDREW

Eoin McAndrew is a Northern Irish playwright based in London. Eoin's work has been performed by the Royal Court, Soho Theatre, Theatre503 and the Royal Shakespeare Company. His first play, *The Girl Who Was Very Good at Lying*, ran at Jermyn Street Theatre and Omnibus Theatre, before opening at the Edinburgh Festival Fringe. His second, *Little Brother*, won the 2024 Verity Bargate Award and was staged at Soho Theatre. His play, *Russell*, was chosen as one of the RSC's 37 Plays and performed at Stratford-upon-Avon. He is an alumnus of the Royal Court International Playwriting Group and the BBC Comedy Writers Room.

Other Titles in this Series

Chris Bush
THE ASSASSINATION OF KATIE HOPKINS
　with Matt Winkworth
THE CHANGING ROOM
CHRIS BUSH PLAYS: ONE
A DOLL'S HOUSE *after* Ibsen
FAUSTUS: THAT DAMNED WOMAN
HUNGRY
JANE EYRE *after* Brontë
THE LAST NOËL
OTHERLAND
ROBIN HOOD AND THE
　CHRISTMAS HEIST
　with Matt Winkworth
ROCK / PAPER / SCISSORS
STANDING AT THE SKY'S EDGE
　with Richard Hawley
STEEL

Jez Butterworth
THE FERRYMAN
THE HILLS OF CALIFORNIA
JERUSALEM
JEZ BUTTERWORTH PLAYS: ONE
JEZ BUTTERWORTH PLAYS: TWO
MOJO
THE NIGHT HERON
PARLOUR SONG
THE RIVER
THE WINTERLING

Caryl Churchill
BLUE HEART
CHURCHILL PLAYS: THREE
CHURCHILL PLAYS: FOUR
CHURCHILL PLAYS: FIVE
CHURCHILL: SHORTS
CLOUD NINE
DING DONG THE WICKED
A DREAM PLAY *after* Strindberg
DRUNK ENOUGH TO SAY I LOVE YOU?
ESCAPED ALONE
FAR AWAY
GLASS. KILL. BLUEBEARD'S FRIENDS.
　IMP.
HERE WE GO
HOTEL
ICECREAM
LIGHT SHINING IN BUCKINGHAMSHIRE
LOVE AND INFORMATION
MAD FOREST
A NUMBER
PIGS AND DOGS
SEVEN JEWISH CHILDREN
THE SKRIKER
THIS IS A CHAIR
THYESTES *after* Seneca
TRAPS
WHAT IF IF ONLY

Caitríona Daly
DUCK DUCK GOOSE
THE LUNCH PUNCH POWER HOUR IN
　CONFERENCE ROOM 4

Stacey Gregg
LAGAN
OVERRIDE
PERVE
SCORCH
SHIBBOLETH
WHEN COWS GO BOOM

Deirdre Kinahan
CROSSINGS
DEIRDRE KINAHAN: SHORTS
HALCYON DAYS
MOMENT
RAGING: THREE PLAYS/SEVEN YEARS
　OF WARFARE IN IRELAND
RATHMINES ROAD
THE SAVIOUR
SPINNING
THE UNMANAGEABLE SISTERS
　after Michel Tremblay

Lucy Kirkwood
BEAUTY AND THE BEAST
　with Katie Mitchell
BLOODY WIMMIN
THE CHILDREN
CHIMERICA
HEDDA *after* Ibsen
THE HUMAN BODY
IT FELT EMPTY WHEN THE HEART
　WENT AT FIRST BUT IT IS
　ALRIGHT NOW
LUCY KIRKWOOD PLAYS: ONE
MOSQUITOES
NSFW
RAPTURE
TINDERBOX
THE WELKIN

Lisa McGee
GIRLS AND DOLLS
NINETEEN NINETY-TWO

Jack Thorne
2ND MAY 1997
AFTER LIFE *after* Hirokazu Kore-eda
BUNNY
BURYING YOUR BROTHER IN
　THE PAVEMENT
A CHRISTMAS CAROL *after* Dickens
THE END OF HISTORY...
HOPE
JACK THORNE PLAYS: ONE
JACK THORNE PLAYS: TWO
JUNKYARD
LET THE RIGHT ONE IN
　after John Ajvide Lindqvist
THE MOTIVE AND THE CUE
MYDIDAE
THE SOLID LIFE OF SUGAR WATER
STACY & FANNY AND FAGGOT
WHEN WINSTON WENT TO WAR WITH
　THE WIRELESS
WHEN YOU CURE ME
WOYZECK *after* Büchner

debbie tucker green
BORN BAD
DEBBIE TUCKER GREEN PLAYS: ONE
DIRTY DUTTERFLY
EAR FOR EYE
HANG
NUT
A PROFOUNDLY AFFECTIONATE,
　PASSIONATE DEVOTION TO
　SOMEONE (– *NOUN*)
RANDOM
STONING MARY
TRADE & GENERATIONS
TRUTH AND RECONCILIATION

Eoin McAndrew

LITTLE BROTHER

NICK HERN BOOKS
London
www.nickhernbooks.co.uk

A Nick Hern Book

Little Brother first published in Great Britain as a paperback original in 2025 by Nick Hern Books Limited, The Glasshouse, 49a Goldhawk Road, London W12 8QP, in association with Soho Theatre, London

Little Brother copyright © 2025 Eoin McAndrew

Eoin McAndrew has asserted his right to be identified as the author of this work

Front cover: photograph by Christine Andrews

Designed and typeset by Nick Hern Books, London
Printed in Great Britain by Mimeo Ltd, Huntingdon, Cambridgeshire PE29 6XX

A CIP catalogue record for this book is available from the British Library

ISBN 978 1 83904 484 7

CAUTION All rights whatsoever in this play are strictly reserved. Requests to reproduce the text in whole or in part should be addressed to the publisher. This book may not be used, in whole or in part, for the development or training of artificial intelligence technologies or systems.

Amateur Performing Rights Applications for performance, including readings and excerpts, by amateurs in the English language throughout the world should be addressed to the Performing Rights Department, Nick Hern Books, The Glasshouse, 49a Goldhawk Road, London W12 8QP, *tel* +44 (0)20 8749 4953, *email* rights@nickhernbooks.co.uk, except as follows:

Australia: ORiGiN Theatrical, Level 1, 213 Clarence Street, Sydney NSW 2000, *tel* +61 (2) 8514 5201, *email* enquiries@originmusic.com.au, *web* www.origintheatrical.com.au

New Zealand: Play Bureau, 20 Rua Street, Mangapapa, Gisborne, 4010, *tel* +64 21 258 3998, *email* info@playbureau.com

USA and Canada: Casarotto Ramsay and Associates Ltd, see details below

Professional Performing Rights Applications for performance by professionals in any medium and in any language throughout the world (including by stock companies in the USA and Canada) should be addressed to Casarotto Ramsay and Associates Ltd, *email* rights@casarotto.co.uk, www.casarotto.co.uk

No performance of any kind may be given unless a licence has been obtained. Applications should be made before rehearsals begin. Publication of this play does not necessarily indicate its availability for performance.

www.nickhernbooks.co.uk/environmental-policy

Nick Hern Books' authorised representative in the EU is
Easy Access System Europe – Mustamäe tee 50, 10621 Tallinn, Estonia
email gpsr.requests@easproject.com

LITTLE BROTHER
by Eoin McAndrew

First performed on 17 October 2025 at Soho Theatre, London

CAST

Niall	Cormac McAlinden
Brigid	Catherine Rees
Michael Doran	Conor O'Donnell
Doctor/Counsellor/Mum/Jackie	Laura Dos Santos

CREATIVES

Director	Emma Jordan
Set and Costume Designer	Zoë Hurwtiz
Lighting Designer	Bethany Gupwell
Sound Designer and Composer	Katie Richardson
Associate Sound Designer	George Sloan
Casting Director	Áine O'Sullivan
Movement Director	Rakhee Sharma
Costume Supervisor	Ellen Rey de Castro
Assistant Director	Millie Foy
Production Manager	Chloe Stally-Gibson
Company Stage Manager	Julia Nimmo
Deputy Stage Manager	Abi Morris
Assistant Stage Manager	Erik Delin

About Soho Theatre

Soho Theatre is London's most vibrant producer of new theatre, comedy and cabaret. A charity and social enterprise, we're driven by a passion for working with bold stories and distinctive artists, connecting them with audiences in original style and creating memorable nights out.

From our early roots in the radical 1970s Soho Poly, we've grown – and grown – from a tiny fringe space into a widely influential cultural organisation operating across our four London performance spaces; through international touring and collaborations with India and elsewhere; as festival regulars from Edinburgh Festival Fringe to Melbourne International Comedy; and filming shows and creating our own digital work seen across social platforms and inflight.

Alongside working with some of the most exciting theatre-makers and comedians in the world, we also nurture the next generation of artists through a thriving range of artist and talent development programmes, artists under commission and in development, and two new writing awards including UK's longest established playwriting prize, the Verity Bargate Award.

In 2025 we're celebrating 25 years at our central London venue Soho Theatre – described by Phoebe Waller-Bridge as the 'the mothership of new artists', Ryan Calais Cameron as 'a major launchpad' and Bryony Kimmings as 'an extraordinary place for people whose work is genre pushing' – whilst opening London's newest venue, the 'jaw-dropping 1000-seat new theatre' (*Time Out*), Soho Theatre Walthamstow in May 2025.

sohotheatre.com I @sohotheatre I @sohotheatreindia

About the Verity Bargate Award

Since its early roots in the Soho Poly, Soho Theatre has always championed new writing – from lunch time plays in the 1970s to today's commissions, attachments, artist and talent development programmes and awards. Launched in 1982, and honouring our organisation's co-founder, the Verity Bargate Award is the longest established playwriting award in the UK and Soho Theatre's flagship playwriting competition. It is also the only playwriting award to guarantee the winning play a fully staged production. The most recent, *Boys on the Verge of Tears* by Sam Grabiner, received an Olivier Award earlier this year.

The Verity Bargate Award, a biennial award open to new and emerging writers in UK and Ireland, is judged by a panel of industry experts – most recently Anupama Chandrasekhar, Alan Cumming, Moira Buffini, Ryan Calais Cameron, Anthony Lau, Rebecca Lucy Taylor AKA Self Esteem – and chaired by Stephen Garret, founder and Executive Chairman of the multi-award-winning production company, and sponsor of the award, Character 7. Previous winners and nominees include Nathan Ellis (*Super High Resolution* at Soho Theatre, 2022), Amanda Wilkin (*Shedding a Skin* at Soho Theatre, 2021 & 2022), Matt Charman (*Bridge of Spies*), Vicky Jones (*Touch* at Soho Theatre, 2019), Toby Whithouse (*Doctor Who*) and many, many more.

From over 1700 entries, Eoin McAndrew is the current Verity Bargate Award winner for his play *Little Brother*, receiving a cash prize, a full London run of the play at Soho Theatre (17 October to 22 November 2025) and, for the first time in the history of the Award, workshops and readings of the play in India and USA. This is a career-defining opportunity to build new relationships outside of the UK and for the play to receive international exposure, building on Soho Theatre's mission to develop sustained cultural exchange with global partners.

The Verity Bargate Award will return in 2026, with submissions opening in January.

SOHO THEATRE STAFF

EXECUTIVE

CEO & Executive Director
Mark Godfrey

Co-Executive Director
Sam Hansford

Interim Chief Operating Officer
Lucy Oliver-Harrison

Fundraising and Partnerships Director
Bhavita Bhatt

Executive Assistant
Annie Jones

TRUSTEES

Chair
Dame Heather Rabbatts DBE

Board Members
Nicholas Allott OBE, David Aukin, Farzana Baduel, Lucy Davies, Martin Esom, Hani Farsi, Campbell Glennie, Lornette Harley, Fawn James, Shaparak Khorsandi, Kate Mayne, David Reitman

SENIOR TEAM

Co-Creative Directors
Steve Lock (Comedy)
Jessica Draper (Creative Engagement)
Rose Abderabbani (Theatre Programme)

Co-Audience & Communications Directors
Peter Flynn & Kelly Fogarty

Head of Food & Beverage
Kim Beeching

Assistant to Creative Heads
Lola Ferguson

TEAMS

Theatre
Eve Allin, Alessandro Babalola, Max Elton, Daljinder Johal, David Luff, Paul Sirett, Pooja Sivaraman, Maddie Wilson

Comedy
Kathryn Craigmyle, Lee Griffiths, Jet Vevers

Creative Engagement
Jenny Bakst, Jules Haworth, Shazad Khalid, Déviniat Adedibu

Press & PR
Augustin Wecxsteen, Ruby Willis, Lou Doyle

Marketing
Kia Noakes, Val Londono Cardona, Alicia Bridge, Flo Granger

Graphic Design
Conor Jatter, Ludmila Bogatchek

Digital
Rhys Matthews, Laura-Inès Wilson, Jody Davies

Audience & Sales
Mariko Primarolo, Jack Cook, Fuad Ahammed, Lainey Alexander, Kitty Smith, Luke Talboys, Sophie Greaves

Operations
Paul Symes, Em Carr, Dee Lindo, Luca Newman

Technical
Stefan Andrews, Amy Whitby-Baker, Rob Johnson, Ben Goodwin, Tom Younger, Elle Kilcullen, Charlie Leslie, Lydia Edwards

Audience Team Soho
Mischa Alexander, Erol Arguden, Brenton Arrendell, Farah Ashraf, Aiyana Bartlett, Ellie Bibby, Auriella Campolina, Becca Carr, Geri Carr, Bronya Doyle, Ben Falacci, Gabriel Harris, Oscar Holloway, Andrew Houghton, Hana Jennings, Lee King-Brown, Tilly Marples, Faith Martin, Kit Miles, Benji Morris, Paul Murphy, Fiona Oakley, Jack Parry, Janisha Perera, Jesse Phillippi, Rosie Revan, Fash Rokey, Alexis Sakellaris, Genevieve Sabherwal, Genevieve Sinha, Johnie Spillane, Sami Sumaria, Dylan Sweet, Abby Timms, Lauren Tranter, Jade Warner-Clayton, Joanne Williams, Eilis Woods

Soho Theatre Bar
Rishay Naidoo, Damian Regan, Cazz Regan, MD Ridoy Khan, Sneha Adhikari, Simon Berry, Megan Chloe Bowles, Emma Brunet Campain de Bony de Lavergne, Sofia Dixon, Lauryn Louise Giovanni, Bibin Gopi, Madeleine Hilton, Abin Marson, Zara Mehrban, Tayafur Rahman, Caleb Seed, Sian Clare Walsh, Chi Whon Won, Zaza Wright

SOHO THEATRE SUPPORTERS

Principal Supporters
Denzil Fernande
Hedley and Fiona Goldberg
Michael and Isobel Holland
Linda Keenan
Soho Circle

Supporting Partners
Matthew Bunting
Stephen Garrett
Angela Hyde-Courtney
Phil & Jane Radcliff
Jonathan Rees

Corporate Sponsors
Adnams Southwold
Bargate Murray
Cameron Mackintosh
Character Seven
Financial Express
NBC Universal International Studios
Oberon Books Ltd
Soho Estates

Trusts & Foundations
The 29th May 1961 Charitable Trust
The Andor Charitable Trust
Bloomberg Philanthropies
Bruce Wake Charitable Trust
The Boris Karloff Charitable Foundation
The Boshier-Hinton Foundation
Chapman Charitable Trust
The Charlotte Bonham-Carter Charitable Trust
The D'Oyly Carte Charitable Trust
Dominic Webber Trust – Core Values
The Fenton Arts Trust
Fidelio Charitable Trust
Garrick Charitable Trust
The Goldsmiths' Company
Harold Hyam Wingate Foundation
Hyde Park Place Estate Charity
The Ian Mactaggart Trust
The Idlewild Trust
The John Thaw Foundation
John Lyon's Charity
KKL Charity
The Kobler Trust
Lara Atkin Charitable Foundation
The Leche Trust
The Mackintosh Foundation
Mohamed S. Farsi Foundation
#My Westminster Fund
Noel Coward Foundation
The Peggy Ramsay Foundation
The Rose Foundation
The Royal Victoria Hall Foundation
Santander Foundation
Schroder Charity Trust
The St James's Piccadilly Charity
Tallow Chandlers Benevolent Fund
The Teale Charitable Trust
The Thistle Trust
Unity Theatre Charitable Trust

Soho Theatre Performance Friends
Ali Braithwaite
Anna Bordon
Amanda Rajkumar
Helen Evans
Bhags Sharma
Rich Thorpe
Chris Thomas
Gary Wilder

Soho Theatre Playwright Friends
Maital Dar
Mrs Emily Fletcher
Liam Goddard
Andrew Lucas
Emma Whitting

LITTLE BROTHER

Characters

BRIGID
NIALL
MICHAEL DORAN
DOCTOR
COUNSELLOR
MUM
JACKIE

Notes

Dialogue in brackets can be whispered, muttered, asides, thrown away.

Dialogue should be delivered quickly, often overlapping.

None of these characters cry.

This text went to press before the end of rehearsals and so may differ slightly from the play as performed.

Belfast. 3 a.m.

A phone is ringing.

NIALL is alone, by the river, with a blue plastic bag.

He shivers.

The phone rings for a long time.

And just as it's about to ring off –

BRIGID	Hello?
	–
	Hello?
NIALL	Heya.
BRIGID	Hello?
NIALL	Hiya. Yeah it's me. Hi.
BRIGID	Niall?
NIALL	Yeah hi. How's you?
BRIGID	What's wrong?
NIALL	What? Nothing. How's things with you? What's up?
BRIGID	What?
	What do you mean what's up? What does that – Ugh one second.
	(No, it's fine. It's my wee brother. He's / just –)
NIALL	Hello? Brigid?
BRIGID	(*Snaps*.) Yes! One second!
	(Just go back to bed. It's fine.)

NIALL	Brigid are you still there?
BRIGID	Yes, I'm here. Just let me – I'm going into another room here –
	Right.
	What is it Niall? Why are you calling?
NIALL	Shit were you asleep?
BRIGID	It's what – It's three in the morning so yes, yes I was asleep.
NIALL	Ah to be fair that's my bad, sorry.
BRIGID	Was there something specific you wanted to talk about, Niall?
NIALL	Yeah. Yes actually.
	I was gonna ask you something but it seems really stupid now that I've gone and woken you up and everything.
BRIGID	Go on.
NIALL	It's kinda –
BRIGID	Just ask me.
NIALL	Well.
	Like I said, it feels really stupid now but.
	Do you know the words to the song that goes like:
	Duh duh-duh-duh duh duh duh duh
	Duh duh-duh-duh duh duh duh duh
	Dah Dah, Dah Dah
	You know that one?
BRIGID	Are you drunk?
NIALL	No.

BRIGID	Where are you?
NIALL	I'm at home.
BRIGID	You sound like you're outside.
NIALL	Nope.
BRIGID	Listen, has something happened or – ?
NIALL	No! Nothing's happened! Nothing's wrong. Everything's fine. I'm fine. I just wanted to talk. I mean Jesus Christ we talk sometimes / don't we?
BRIGID	At three in the / morning?
NIALL	Well remember I try to call you during the day but you're / at work and you get mad at me –
BRIGID	I'm putting the phone down.
NIALL	Don't do that. Don't hang up.
	–
	Brigid. Please. Come on.
	Tell me how you are. Come on.
BRIGID	–
	(*Deeply unimpressed.*) I'm fine.
NIALL	Good. That's good.
	How's work?
BRIGID	Fine.
NIALL	And your course?
BRIGID	It's fine.
NIALL	And how's things just generally?
BRIGID	All fine.
NIALL	Well see, aren't you glad we had this talk?

BRIGID	Niall, we can talk in the morning.
NIALL	Are you mad at me?
BRIGID	No.
NIALL	Are you sure? Because I can't see your face but from the tone of your voice –
BRIGID	I've just told you that I'm not mad.
NIALL	Sure.
BRIGID	Although I will admit –
NIALL	Oh.
BRIGID	That I am currently.
	Unimpressed.
NIALL	Right.
BRIGID	And I think that calling someone up this late at night for no real reason is a little bit inconsiderate. Would you not agree with that assessment?
NIALL	D'you have someone round tonight?
BRIGID	What? No. Why? No.
NIALL	I just thought that maybe you had someone round.
BRIGID	No, I don't 'have anyone round'. D'you want to know any more Niall or am I free to go back to / sleep?
NIALL	Oh fuck.
	He's seen something.
BRIGID	Niall?
NIALL	Oh fuck. Shit.
BRIGID	What? Niall?
NIALL	Oh shit. Oh my god. Oh my god.

BRIGID	What's happening? Are you okay?
NIALL	Oh fucking hell / oh my god oh my god.
BRIGID	Niall talk to me, what is it? What's happening?
NIALL	Ah man.
	Oh no. Wait. Ah. No.
BRIGID	Niall? What is it?
NIALL	It's nothing.
	Sorry.
	I thought I saw a swan.
BRIGID	A swan?
NIALL	Yeah, you know, a swan. Like the bird.
	I thought I saw one, but it was just a plastic bag.
BRIGID	Fuck's sake.
	You said you were at home.
NIALL	I am. Yeah.
	What happened was I saw what I thought was a swan through the window but fuckin'…
	Alas. You know?
BRIGID	–
	Niall, d'you need money?
	Is that what this is?
NIALL	What? No.
	(No I don't need money I wasn't calling to ask for money I'm not –)
	He paces, walking away from the phone.

BRIGID	Niall?
	Niall are you there?
	Picks up the phone again.
NIALL	Hi. Yep.
BRIGID	If you can hear me then answer me when I talk to you.
NIALL	I don't need money. I wasn't calling to ask you for money.
BRIGID	And you're. You know, you're okay and everything?
NIALL	Yeah.
BRIGID	How's things with you and – um…
NIALL	Natalie.
BRIGID	Natalie yeah. How's Natalie?
NIALL	Good. Really good actually. She's the best.
BRIGID	That's nice. And work?
NIALL	Great. Same. You know?
BRIGID	And you're okay right?
	You're fine?
	He goes to say something. Doesn't.
NIALL	Yeah, I'm fine.
	Listen, I'm sorry. I couldn't sleep and I wanted to chat to someone and I dunno –
	I wanted to hear your voice.
	It was stupid.
BRIGID	–
	That's alright.
	What're you doing Saturday?

NIALL	Saturday? Let me just think.
	Em. I'm free. Why?
BRIGID	How about we meet up, we go for a wee walk? How's that?
NIALL	–
	Saturday?
BRIGID	Yeah. What d'you think?
NIALL	I can do that.
BRIGID	Okay. That's a plan then.
	I'll message you in the week.
NIALL	Sure.
BRIGID	And I'll see you Saturday.
	Get some sleep.
NIALL	Yep.
	Bye.

She hangs up.

Long pause.

NIALL *sits. Shivers.*

He takes a little bottle of lighter fluid out of his bag.

He douses his right hand in it.

He takes out a box of matches.

He lights one.

He sets fire to his right hand.

+ 3 hours

A hospital corridor.

Plastic chairs and a water fountain.

BRIGID *and a* DOCTOR.

DOCTOR	Would you like me to repeat anything I've just said?
BRIGID	(*For a moment, she genuinely doesn't understand the question.*) Uh.
	No.
DOCTOR	Can I get you some water or anything?
BRIGID	I'm fine.
DOCTOR	Shall I continue?
	So your brother's hand is quite badly burned, but thankfully not enough to require skin grafts. He's with the nurse now, who's cleaning the wound, removing dirt and dead tissue.
BRIGID	(dead tissue)
DOCTOR	That's right. Then they're going to bandage his hand. It sounds like the fire went out relatively quickly and didn't travel very far up his arm. That's a good thing.
	It could have been a lot worse than it ended up being.
BRIGID	Can I see him?

DOCTOR	Like I said, he's with the nurse now, but you'll get to see him very shortly.
	Would you like me to repeat any part of what we've just talked about?
BRIGID	Not um.
	Not right now I don't think.
DOCTOR	Of course.
	Are you sure I can't get you any water?
BRIGID	No, I don't want any water.
DOCTOR	Okay.
	–
	Do you mind if I get myself some water?
BRIGID	That'd be fine.

The DOCTOR *pours herself a cup of water.*

She sits and has a sip and does a little 'ah'.

DOCTOR	The water's really good here. I don't know why.

Pause.

BRIGID	So he can just… go?
DOCTOR	We'll keep him in for a little while longer, but you'll be able to take him home today.
	It might be best if he isn't left by himself for too long. Does he have anywhere that he can…?
BRIGID	–
	He can stay with me. (I'll work something out.)

DOCTOR	Is there anyone else that needs to hear this, or that you'd like to call?
BRIGID	Like?
DOCTOR	Family. Usually. Is there any other family that should know? Parents or – ?
BRIGID	Can I –
	Can I get back to you on that?
DOCTOR	Of course.
BRIGID	Oh and his girlfriend. She should probably – I should call her shouldn't I?
DOCTOR	That sounds good. What's her name?
BRIGID	I.
	I don't remember.
	It's like Lois or something?
	I just don't remember.
DOCTOR	That's alright.
	He's going to have to come back in day after tomorrow just so that we can check on the wound. I'll prescribe a cream that'll need to be applied once a day and bandages will need to change every two days. I'll talk you through how to administer / the cream –
BRIGID	Wait wait wait.
	BRIGID *takes a scrap of paper and a pen from her bag.*
	She writes down everything.
	Come back in the day after tomorrow. Cream on once a day.
DOCTOR	And bandages –

BRIGID	Every two days.
DOCTOR	Me and Niall have had a little chat and I'm gonna prescribe some medication. Something for the pain and we've talked about antidepressants.
	I'll also write a letter of referral to the community mental health and fire team. I'll talk you both through that in more detail later.
BRIGID	Okay.
DOCTOR	I'm going to recommend counselling. Now the waiting list is very long, so I'd say we should get Niall on that as soon as possible.
	We'll also refer him to an S-I-S-P-G. I'll contact them on Niall's behalf and then they should be in touch. Does that all sound alright?
BRIGID	An S-I-S...?
DOCTOR	A self-immolation support and prevention group.
BRIGID	There's a support group for.
	People who try and set themselves on fire?
DOCTOR	Yes.
BRIGID	Does this kind of thing. Happen a lot then?
	So much so that there's a support group for people who set themselves / on fire?
DOCTOR	Ooh. Sorry. I'd steer you away from calling them 'people who set themselves on fire'.

BRIGID	Sorry?
DOCTOR	We try to say 'people who *have* set themselves on fire'. Generally, I think it's best to talk about destructive behaviours rather than to suggest that the behaviour is ingrained in that person.
BRIGID	Uh-huh.
DOCTOR	I know it's a little thing, but I think the terminology we use around this is really important.
BRIGID	This is a – a – thing that people do?
DOCTOR	Sadly.
	Unfortunately, Northern Ireland has one of the highest rates of people setting themselves on fire in Europe.
	In fact, more people have set fire to themselves in the last twenty years, than in the preceding *forty* years.
	It's all explained very well in this leaflet.
	The DOCTOR *hands* BRIGID *a leaflet, which she stares at limply.*
	Now, going forward: over the next few days I'd just try and keep his mind off it. Try not to leave him alone very often. I appreciate this might be difficult with work.
BRIGID	I'll – I don't know. I'll sort something.
DOCTOR	What is it you do?
BRIGID	Civil service.
DOCTOR	(*Sympathetically.*) Ah.
	This may sound overcautious, but I'd avoid watching any films or television

	shows that feature people getting set on fire or burning alive. Niall might find those upsetting.
BRIGID	Are there a lot of those?
DOCTOR	More than you'd think.
	Towering Inferno. Carrie. The Thing. Some of the *Saw* films, I think. These are just off the top of my head. There's probably loads more. Oh anything set in hell. You get the picture.
BRIGID	I get it.
DOCTOR	Or like *Apocalypse Now*. Have you seen *Apocalypse Now*?
BRIGID	No.
DOCTOR	Oh it's incredible. Don't watch it.
	And I'd take anything flammable out of your home.
BRIGID	Anything?
DOCTOR	Flammable.
BRIGID	Right.
DOCTOR	Or anything that could potentially be used to start a fire. For now, at least.
	So that's lighters, matches…
BRIGID	Of course.
DOCTOR	Candles. Fire lighters. That sort of thing.
	Hair straighteners. Heat lamps. Hot plates. Coal. Flint. Barbecues.
	Do you have a gas oven?
BRIGID	Electric.

DOCTOR	That'll be fine.
	Petrol. Aerosols. Flares. Flare guns. Loose, dry leaves. A powerful magnifying glass. No spray deodorants because he might do that thing where you hold a lighter and you can / make a –
	BRIGID *has stopped writing.*
BRIGID	What the fuck are you talking about?
DOCTOR	Excuse me?
BRIGID	This is fucking insane. Flare guns? What the fuck are you talking about?
DOCTOR	No of course. I understand this is a lot / and I apologise if it came across –
BRIGID	Jesus Christ you're just sitting there like like like this is normal like this is –
	This isn't real.
	What the fuck was he thinking?
DOCTOR	I don't think it'll be helpful to think of it as his fault.
BRIGID	Oh I'm sorry then whose fault is it?
DOCTOR	Maybe 'fault' wasn't the right word –
BRIGID	Is it your fault?
DOCTOR	No I wouldn't say it was my fault –
BRIGID	Well if it's not his fault, or yours and I don't think it's mine then whose fucking fault is it?
	You know? Because these things don't just happen. This isn't real. People would be doing something if this was – it's not like a naturally occurring force of – people set themselves on fire.

>
> You're telling me that people set themselves on fire like all the time now and we don't know why and we can't stop them from doing it. So it makes me think who the *fuck's* fault is that?
>
> You know?
>
> Who – like –
>
> I –
>
> You know?
>
> –
>
> Sorry.
>
> I'm sorry.
>
> I'm calm now. I'm calm. I'm sorry.

DOCTOR: That's alright.

BRIGID: No it isn't. You probably have other people to see.

DOCTOR: I mean. Yes.

> –
>
> Wait here.
>
> *The* DOCTOR *gets a cup of water from the machine.*
>
> *She passes it to* BRIGID, *who drinks.*

BRIGID: That's actually / really good.

DOCTOR: The water's really good here. / I don't know why.

BRIGID: It's like fresher or something.

> –
>
> Why would he do something like this?

DOCTOR	I don't think it's helpful for me to speculate.
	You can ask him, I just don't know that you'll find the answer comforting at this point.
	BRIGID *takes another drink. Crumples up the cup.*
BRIGID	I'm sorry I snapped at you.
	That's not how I talk. In normal circumstances I'm very nice.
DOCTOR	I've heard worse.
	–
	I think you're going to need to take care of yourself over the next stage of this.
	Your brother's going to need an awful lot of support, and we don't want this to happen again.
BRIGID	It won't.
DOCTOR	Pardon?
BRIGID	It won't happen again.

+ 2 days

Brigid's flat.

BRIGID *and* NIALL.

NIALL *has a rucksack, and his hand is in a tidy white bandage.*

BRIGID and on the Friday I'll work from home a bit but I'll just have my laptop open and you can just – Oh. One thing: please don't touch the oven when I'm not here. If you're hungry, there's plenty of stuff that can be microwaved and – towels! I don't know if you remembered to bring towels at all, but if you didn't there's towels over there in the cupboard, so no need to worry about. Towels.

This can be fun. 'Cause when's the last time we lived together? You'd have been what – eleven, twelve?

We can go for walks in the park and we can watch films and you could choose the films.

We could go swimming!

Wouldn't that be good?

When was the last time you just went swimming, you know?

I don't suppose you brought any swimming stuff, did you?

–

Niall?

NIALL	Hm?
BRIGID	Did you bring any swimming stuff?
NIALL	No.
BRIGID	Ah well.
	Probably not the best idea. What with the –
	She points at his burned hand, immediately regrets it.
NIALL	What's that?
BRIGID	–
	It's a smoke alarm.
NIALL	Did you always have one there?
BRIGID	I got some extra smoke alarms.
	One for each room. Gotta be safe.
	NIALL *nods*.
NIALL	What's in there?
	He points to a plastic container on the floor.
	He goes over to it.
BRIGID	That is – actually that shouldn't even be here because that is –
	That's just some stuff that I'm getting rid of.
NIALL	Lighters. Matches. Candles.
BRIGID	Okay full disclosure.
	Those are all the things in my flat that could start a fire.
	Except the oven.
	Which you shouldn't touch unless / I'm here.

NIALL	Which I shouldn't touch unless you're here. Got it.
BRIGID	I'm gonna make a coffee. You want one?
NIALL	No.
BRIGID	–

There are a few rules, for living here.

We're gonna talk, every day, me and you, and you can just tell me how you're feeling that day – on a scale of one to ten if that's helpful. That's rule one.

And I'm going to check that you've taken your medication. Every day. Not because I don't trust you, but because… Because.

And the last rule is, when I ask you something, I need you to be honest with me. Is that fair?

And I know that that sounds like a lot of rules, but we can make this fun.

I don't know how yet, but we can.

–

I love you.

NIALL *doesn't look at her.*

NIALL	Did you tell Mum?
BRIGID	No.

NIALL *nods.*

Do you need to call your work and tell them you won't be in for a while?

–

Niall?

NIALL	No.
BRIGID	Why not?
NIALL	Because.
BRIGID	Because what?
	—
	Right.
	(I thought that might be the –)
	And when did that happen?
NIALL	A little while ago.
BRIGID	Okay.
	Well, do you need to call…?
	Sorry, what is her / name?
NIALL	Natalie.
BRIGID	Natalie. Right. D'you not need to call Natalie?
	She'll be worried about you. You should tell her that you're staying here.
	D'you not think?
NIALL	I don't need to call Natalie.
BRIGID	Is that – ?
	NIALL *nods*.
	And when did that…?
	I'm a bit confused here Niall because on the phone the other night you said that work was going well.
NIALL	Uh-huh.
BRIGID	And then I asked about Natalie and you said that things were going good.

	That's right isn't it, or am I getting this completely wrong?
NIALL	I was lying then.
BRIGID	Okay. Why did you lie?
	NIALL *shrugs*.
	Right well I don't really understand that.
	But at least this is making a bit more sense to me now.
NIALL	How?
BRIGID	Well, you'd lost your job, you and Natalie had broken up, you were upset –
	NIALL *goes to say something*.
	We don't have to talk about it now.
	For the next week, it's just you and me.
	Coffee!
	She goes to leave, turns back.
	I'd really like you to do something for me.
	I'd like you to promise me that you're not going to try and set yourself on fire again.
NIALL	I promise I'm not going to try and set myself on fire again.
BRIGID	Good.
	Okay then.
	I'm glad we've got this sorted.
	She goes to leave, turns back.
	One last rule.
	Most important rule actually.

	If you *ever* feel like that. Or feel like you're going to do that again.
	You call me.
	Do you understand?
	I will be so upset and so mad if you don't do that.
	Any time, any place.
	You call me. Right?
NIALL	–
	I mean.
	I did.
BRIGID	What?
NIALL	I did call you.
BRIGID	–
	Right.
	You did.
	I'll get that coffee then.

+ 4 days

Brigid's flat.

BRIGID *and* NIALL.

BRIGID	I got you something.
NIALL	What?
	She throws him some sticky notes.
	Sticky notes.
BRIGID	Sticky notes.
	So the last couple of days, you've just been sleeping a lot, and that's great, but I'm going back to work next week, and I think it would be really good for you to make a plan while I'm here to help you do it.
	D'you ever make lists?
NIALL	I don't even understand the question.
BRIGID	I make a lot of lists. Just to like organise my thoughts and have them all spread out in front of me, and suddenly everything's just that little bit more manageable. Just like one, two, three –
NIALL	I understand the concept of a list.
BRIGID	Great.
	First thing on the list, you call the counsellor. That's an easy one – we have the number.

NIALL	Do we have the number?
BRIGID	I looked it up.
	Number one. Call counsellor.
	She writes 'CALL COUNSELLOR' on sticky note.
	Number two. What do you want to say to the counsellor?
NIALL	I don't know.
	'Please help, I'm mental.'
BRIGID	No you're not. Don't say that.
	He rubs his face.
	Okay. I want you to write something nice about yourself on a sticky note.
NIALL	Really?
BRIGID	Write down one thing that you're good at.
	He tries to write something, but with his hand…
NIALL	I can't hold the pen and the thing at the same time –
BRIGID	Oh right.
	She takes the pen and the sticky notes.
	Go on. What are you good at?
NIALL	I don't know that I'm good at anything.
BRIGID	You're good at loads of stuff. You're clever.
NIALL	I'm not clever.
BRIGID	Yes you are.
NIALL	Not actually clever. Not like how you're clever.

BRIGID	Well no. But we're different kinds of clever.
	Come on. Think of something. One good thing.
NIALL	–
	–
	I'm patient.
BRIGID	Are you?
NIALL	Fuck's sake.
BRIGID	Sorry no yeah of course / you are.
NIALL	Not with you, I'm not patient with you but with some people who aren't you, I am patient!
BRIGID	Brilliant. Yes. You are patient.
	She writes 'I AM PATIENT' on a sticky note and sticks it to the wall.
	What else are you good at?
NIALL	I am good at…
BRIGID	Yeah?
NIALL	I am.
	Good at.
	Setting myself on fire like / the big fucking mental mess that I am.
BRIGID	DON'T JOKE ABOUT IT.
NIALL	Jesus Christ. Fine.
BRIGID	I DON'T LIKE IT WHEN YOU JOKE ABOUT IT
NIALL	I'm the one that did it, surely I should be allowed / to make a joke about it.

BRIGID	I don't find it funny. I'm never gonna find it funny. I don't ask you to do a lot but one of the things I ask is that you don't / make jokes about it.
NIALL	Fine! Fine! Fucking hell. I'm sorry, alright?
BRIGID	Don't say sorry – I'm not a monster!
	You're only gonna be here for a month. So we have to, you know, do what we can to make you…
NIALL	More like you?
BRIGID	Better.
	BRIGID*'s phone rings.*
NIALL	Your phone's going.
BRIGID	Yep.
NIALL	You wanna take it?
BRIGID	No.
	We're spending time together.

+ 10 days

Brigid's flat.

NIALL *is talking to a* COUNSELLOR.

COUNSELLOR	Over the last two weeks, how often have you thought or fantasised about setting objects on fire?
NIALL	Some of the time.
COUNSELLOR	Okay.
	Over the last two weeks how often have you felt the impulse to hurt yourself in any way? By this we mean a violent, intrusive thought.
NIALL	–
	Um.
COUNSELLOR	Do you want me to repeat the options?
NIALL	Yes please.
COUNSELLOR	The options are: At no time. Some of the time. Slightly less than half of the time. More than half of the time. Most of the time.
NIALL	Then.
	Slightly less than half the time.
COUNSELLOR	Okay.
	Over the last two weeks, how often have you felt like you're a failure, or that you're letting loved ones down?

NIALL	I don't know.
	All the time.
COUNSELLOR	Okay.
	I'll put that as 'Most of the time'.
	Last one: over the last two weeks, how often have you felt the impulse to set yourself or part of yourself on fire?
NIALL	Slightly less than half the time.
COUNSELLOR	Okay.
	That's it. You can breathe now.
	He exhales. They both laugh a little.
	He's a bit shaky.
	Thank you for doing that for me, Niall.
	How do you feel now?
NIALL	A bit – you know?
COUNSELLOR	Of course. Take a moment.
NIALL	Thanks.
COUNSELLOR	Can I just ask, have you encountered any side effects from your medication so far?
NIALL	Like what?
COUNSELLOR	It can be lots of different things. Tiredness. Muscle aches. Trouble sleeping.
	You might find they affect you sexually.
NIALL	In what way uh sexually?
COUNSELLOR	You might find they have an effect on your libido. You might have some problems with ejaculation.

NIALL	–
	These pills are gonna make me ejaculate?
COUNSELLOR	Uh. No. No. They might make it more difficult / to.
NIALL	Oh right. I get you.
	Uh no. No side effects.
COUNSELLOR	Good.
	Thank you for going through the survey with me, Niall.
	Now there are quite a few things you've said that give me cause for concern.
NIALL	Right.
COUNSELLOR	But I think this gives us a pretty good idea as to our next steps.
	Based on what you've told me here, I think it's important that we find you a counsellor.
NIALL	–
	What?
COUNSELLOR	Sorry?
NIALL	What do you mean, sorry?
COUNSELLOR	I am going to refer you to a counsellor.
NIALL	You're my counsellor.
COUNSELLOR	Oh. No.
NIALL	What?
COUNSELLOR	Has no one talked you through this?
NIALL	You're not a counsellor?
COUNSELLOR	Well I am a counsellor, but I'm not your counsellor.

NIALL	Then why'd I just tell you all that stuff?
COUNSELLOR	I'm sorry, I thought you understood this.
	I'm just here for the assessment – this conversation is for me to ascertain the severity of your issues and then make a recommendation. Then you'll be placed on a waiting list, and be passed on to a counsellor, once one becomes available.
NIALL	So you're what? You're just a person?
COUNSELLOR	In a way, yes.
NIALL	Okay how long does it take for someone to become available?
COUNSELLOR	I think you'd be looking anywhere between eight to twelve months.
NIALL	But you said I needed one.
COUNSELLOR	Look at it this way: you're making progress, you're on medication, you have a support system in your sister. This might sound harsh, but you're not – at the moment – a priority.
	It's a point system, and this assessment will dictate where you're placed on the waiting list.
NIALL	Let me take the test again, I'll score higher.
COUNSELLOR	Niall –
NIALL	Can't you be my counsellor?
	I like you.
	And I already told you everything and I don't want to start again with a whole new person –

COUNSELLOR	I'm sorry.
NIALL	Right.
COUNSELLOR	Now, that's nearly our time. Is there anything else you'd like to ask before we go?
NIALL	No.
	–
	Okay, yeah.
	How long until I – I don't know – until I feel better?
	Because I don't want to feel like this any more.
	You know?
	And I think about, like, a year from now, and I'm like.
	I can't picture it.
	I can't.
COUNSELLOR	–
	I'm going to tell you something that might be difficult to hear, but I'd really like you to listen to me, because I think it's important that you know this.
	You might well have these thoughts, these feelings, for the rest of your life.
	But Niall.
	The important thing, that I want you to remember is that they are im–
	She freezes.
	Glitchy sound.

NIALL   —

                Hello?

                Sorry I think you've – I think you've frozen?

                Hello? I think your internet has –

                Can you hear me?

                Hello?

                You're frozen. You're frozen.

                He just sits there.

                Glitchy sound.

                COUNSELLOR *unfreezes*.

COUNSELLOR   – always pass. And I think if you can bear that in mind, you're gonna be alright.

                Okay?

NIALL   —

                Sure.

COUNSELLOR   I hope you've found this helpful.

                I'm afraid that's our time.

+ 2 weeks, 3 days

Brigid's flat.

NIALL *is watching a film.*

He's just got to the bit in The Wicker Man *where the villagers set fire to the Wicker Man and that guy says 'Oh Christ! Oh Jesus Christ!'*

BRIGID *comes in from work.*

BRIGID	What are you watching?
NIALL	Oh. It's like a –
BRIGID	Oh my god what are watching?
NIALL	Sorry this was just on / TV but –
BRIGID	Are they gonna set fire to that man?
	Don't look at it! Where's the – where's the thing??
	She grabs the remote. Turns it off.
	Why were you watching that?
NIALL	Oh it was just on TV and I was watching it and – I don't know.
BRIGID	Are you okay?
NIALL	I'm fine.
BRIGID	Did that – I don't know – Set you off?
NIALL	Oh. No.
BRIGID	Good. That's good.
	Why didn't it set you off? I would've thought that that – would be –

NIALL	I guess.
	I didn't even make the connection really.
BRIGID	I'm gonna email someone. They shouldn't be showing stuff like that –
	See yeah – in the description it doesn't mention fire at all, it just says contains nudity, occult themes and horror. Why were you watching this?
NIALL	I'm really fine. You don't need to email anyone.
BRIGID	I mean okay Niall but you're actually not the only one affected by this issue so if not for you –
	–
	Did you know that was gonna happen?
	Did you know that that happened in the film?
NIALL	I mean.
	It's a really famous film.
BRIGID	And you watched it anyway?
NIALL	It's fine!
BRIGID	THEY WERE GOING TO BURN HIM IN A BIG WICKER MAN!
	Is that why you wanted to watch it?
NIALL	No.
BRIGID	Is this what you do while I'm at work? Watch people get burned alive? 'Cause I'll work from home then if you can't be trusted not / to –

NIALL	Not to what? Watch a film?
	BRIGID's phone rings.
	Who's that?
BRIGID	No one.
NIALL	You can answer it if you want.
	She picks it up and declines the call.
BRIGID	I don't want to.
NIALL	Then can I watch the end of the film?
BRIGID	No.
NIALL	Cool.
	I'm gonna go for a walk.
BRIGID	It's night-time.
NIALL	Yep.
BRIGID	Niall, you're being ridiculous.
NIALL	I'll be back in a bit.
BRIGID	You can't leave your phone.
NIALL	I want to.
BRIGID	What if –
NIALL	Can I just do that? Can I just go for a walk? Can I leave my phone down? Can I watch a film? Can I be on my own for like, a second, without you being there?
	BRIGID is furious.
BRIGID	–
	Of course you can.

	Niall. Right now I'm feeling a certain way.
	And I want to express that feeling to you.
	But I don't want to make you upset or make you – spiral. So, be honest, d'you think that you can hear what I have to say and accept it, while also bearing in mind that I'm not saying it to make you feel bad about yourself?
NIALL	–
	Yes.
BRIGID	I think.
	–
NIALL	Yeah?
BRIGID	That you are being a bit annoying.
	And deliberately mischaracterising my attempts to help as me being controlling.
	And.
	That is frustrating to me sometimes.
	Am I okay to – ?
NIALL	Yeah no I love it, keep going.
BRIGID	So I think it would be beneficial, for the rest of the time you're here, if we were easier on each other.
	Because sometimes, you can be… difficult.
NIALL	Absolutely agree.
BRIGID	D'you think that's fair?
NIALL	Completely fair. I'm a fucking piece of shit.

BRIGID	No you're not!
NIALL	I really am!
BRIGID	Don't do that!
NIALL	Don't do what?
BRIGID	Don't be like 'I'm a fuckin scumbag' / or like 'I'm just a fucking worm' when that's not what I'm saying!
NIALL	I am a fucking scumbag!
	I *am* a worm! That is exactly / what I am!
BRIGID	Stop it!
	It's selfish and it's self-pitying and it makes it really fucking hard to be annoyed at you!
NIALL	Sorry.
BRIGID	And don't say sorry!
	He laughs a little.
	What?
NIALL	Just. Funny.
	–
	I'm gonna go for that walk.
BRIGID	Take your phone.
	He takes his phone.

+ 3 weeks, 5 days

Brigid's flat.

From the next room, music and people talking.

NIALL *is alone in the garden.*

BRIGID *comes out, with a bottle of something.*

BRIGID	Yeah one sec!
	Why're you hiding out here?
NIALL	I'm not hiding.
BRIGID	You sure you're okay? You're being quiet. Which is fine. But just checking you're having a good time.
NIALL	I'm having a good time.
BRIGID	Can you open this?
NIALL	Sure.
BRIGID	D'you feel weird at all?
NIALL	No. Why? Am I being weird?
BRIGID	I'm just saying, if you're feeling weird just let me know and we can send everyone home.
NIALL	Your friends are nice.
BRIGID	They are, aren't they?
	What were you guys talking about?
NIALL	Oh, your friend Max was talking to me about the uh German / uh –

BRIGID	The German Democratic Republic?
NIALL	Yes.
BRIGID	The man's obsessed with the German Democratic Republic.
NIALL	Your friends are all really smart.
BRIGID	They're not that smart, they're just loud.
NIALL	Uh Brigid.
BRIGID	What? What is it?
NIALL	Um.
	Your friends. Do they uh, do they know? Like what happened? And why I'm staying here?
BRIGID	They know you've moved in with me. They know you've hurt your hand.
	That's it.
NIALL	Grand.
BRIGID	They like you.
	And Clíodhna just told me she thought you were fit.
NIALL	Clíodhna said that?
	Ha. That's so funny.
	No she didn't. Did she?
BRIGID	She did.
NIALL	And is Clíodhna seeing anyone or –
BRIGID	She's gay.
NIALL	Oh.
	Like, exclusively?
BRIGID	Go on.

	MICHAEL DORAN *appears in the doorway.*
	He's wearing a gilet.
MICHAEL DORAN	Uh. Hello.
BRIGID	Oh. Hi.
	Pause.
NIALL	Hi.
BRIGID	Uh, Niall, this is my friend Michael. Michael this is Niall.
MICHAEL DORAN	Ah, is this your wee brother?
	Alright big man? Michael Doran. How's you?
NIALL	Yeah I'm good.
BRIGID	Niall, d'you want to go in and show them how to work the speaker?
NIALL	Sure.
MICHAEL DORAN	It was nice to meet you.
NIALL	I'm just going in there.
MICHAEL DORAN	Right yeah.
	NIALL *leaves them alone.*
	It's nice to see you.
BRIGID	You too.
MICHAEL DORAN	Oh! I got you a Christmas card.
	It's a wee bit crumpled because it's been in my pocket. Sorry.
BRIGID	Thank you.
MICHAEL DORAN	And you don't need to open it now.
	It just says Merry Christmas and Happy New Year and all that.

BRIGID	That's lovely.
MICHAEL DORAN	And it's nice to finally meet your wee brother.
	How's he doing? Is he well?
BRIGID	He's doing better. He's gonna be moving out soon. He's looking for somewhere.
MICHAEL DORAN	Ah nice. That's really good.
	And listen, sorry I'm so late. There was a bit of traffic and if I'm honest I set off late and so the traffic just sort of compounded / the –
BRIGID	Look I'm sorry that we haven't spoken / in so long.
MICHAEL DORAN	No no no. Don't be. You had to look after your wee brother like.
	I completely. Family. Hundred per cent. You know?
	–
	If anything, it's just like, another good thing about you, you know? That you'd do that and um –
	Is that new?
BRIGID	No, that's always been there.
MICHAEL DORAN	Ah right.
	I actually did write a bit more in the card.
BRIGID	D'you want me to open it now?
MICHAEL DORAN	You don't have to.
BRIGID	I don't mind. I can open it now.
MICHAEL DORAN	No. Uh.

BRIGID	I'll open it.
MICHAEL DORAN	No, don't.
BRIGID	What?
MICHAEL DORAN	Sorry maybe I should take it back actually.
	You don't need to open it.
BRIGID	What's in the card?
MICHAEL DORAN	Nothing's in the card. Give me it back.
BRIGID	Michael.
MICHAEL DORAN	I missed you.
	–
	I missed you. That's what it says in the card. That's all.
BRIGID	Oh.
	I probably don't need to open it now, do I?
MICHAEL DORAN	Probably not, no.
BRIGID	I missed you.
MICHAEL DORAN	Really?
	That's great. That's really good to know.
	Thank you.
	So anyway, how's everything keeping with you?
	She kisses him.
	Music starts to play from the next room.

+ 1 month

Smoke.

Crackling.

And that voice: 'Oh Christ, Oh Jesus Christ'.

BRIGID wakes up, and everything cuts out.

It's the middle of the night and NIALL is standing there.

NIALL	Brigid?
BRIGID	What's wrong?
NIALL	I'm really sorry.
	Can I just – just –
BRIGID	What is it?
NIALL	It's okay actually. Sorry I shouldn't have –
BRIGID	Niall?
NIALL	FUCK.
BRIGID	Hey. Come on.
NIALL	Sorry. Sorry. Can I just be here for a bit?
	I'm just not feeling good at the moment and I –
	I don't know.
	I think I need to be outside or or or with someone else so that –
BRIGID	Breathe.
	What can I do?

NIALL	Fuck I don't know why I'm like this.
BRIGID	Okay, just remember, what are our steps?
NIALL	FUCK.
BRIGID	Okay don't do that. You're okay.
	I'm gonna go get some ice and I'll be right back.
	She goes to leave.
NIALL	No! Can you not go please? **I think something's wrong I think**
	I'm sorry.
BRIGID	Don't be sorry.
	Hold my hand.
	Squeeze my hand. Hard as you want.
	Ow. Not that hard.
NIALL	I'm sorry.
BRIGID	Keep squeezing my hand. You're okay.
NIALL	Can you just talk to me about something?
BRIGID	Like what?
NIALL	I don't know. Anything.
BRIGID	Um okay. So Belfast presents a unique problem in urban planning –
	We don't hear all of it, but we can hear snatches of what he's muttering to himself. Things like 'piece of shit', 'fucking nothing'. BRIGID *keeps holding his hand.*

Nothing. You're fucking nothing, you're just this fucking thing a Thing that makes everything around you turn to shit you don't deserve a single fucking thing you have

NIALL   FUCK.

He tries to rip out a chunk of his hair.

BRIGID   Don't do that, Niall.

> I don't feel good I think I'm gonna be sick I think I'm gonna be sick I want to be sick I'm gonna be sick be sick be sick be sick be sick

He hits himself, hard.

Hey. HEY. **You need to calm down now / This is bad / This is very bad**

Don't do that! Niall, look at me. Look at me. You need to calm down. This isn't good.

Stop it. Stop it. Niall. Calm down.

This is ridiculous.

NIALL   Don't touch me!

BRIGID   I can't let you do that – this is ridiculous now

NIALL   FUCK OFF

Don't fucking touch me

BRIGID   I need to call someone

NIALL   GET THE FUCK

GET OFF ME

~~Get off me~~

DON'T TOUCH ME

~~Get off me~~

Get OUT! OKAY / I DON'T NEED YOU TO

to to to to to **Look at you / You're scaring her**

BRIGID   Niall have you taken your medication have you done that today

she hates you you're ruining her life / she hates you and she's right

NIALL		I can't	**I don't want to be here**
		I can't breathe	**I want to be outside I need to be outside I feel like I'm**
BRIGID		Niall talk to me	**gonna throw up I want to set fire to my hand the side of my head to the side of my head if I do that I'll feel better I want to I'll feel better I'll feel better the side of my head then I'll feel better**

GET I can't breathe I can't breathe can you just shut up SHUT UP can you do that please

I don't want you to see me like this

Niall I need you to listen to me

Fuck I don't know what I'm doing

okay you have to calm down

I can't breathe I can't breathe

hey come on now Niall you're

scaring me

now okay you gotta stop that

my love okay? Breathe. One.

+ 1 MONTH   49

Squeeze my hand. One.

two

Remember the things that the – that the –
    Niall please don't do that I'm asking you okay please don't do that

Two! Yeah you're

doing great

Niall can you remember the things –

Ca**S**T**UP**I**D PIECE OF SHIT YOU'RE FUCKING NOTHING FUCKIN'**

Hey come on you're doing so

Niall please don't do that I'm asking you okay please don't do that

STOP THAT GET OFF

Niall please don't do that

my love okay that's not good

you'll hurt yourself.

Count to five with me okay?

Please can you do that?

NIALL **stop hitting yourself you fucking freak what's wrong with you**   gonna set fire to my fucking hand my face I'm nothing I'm not real it doesn't matter

You're not well you're sick you make people sick you make people sad they'd all be better off

**You're scaring her
You're scaring your
own sister
you stupid**

**I can't
there's something wrong
with me**

come on please

you need to

you
need to need to

**Look at her look at
what you do to
people
this is you**

come on please calm
down my love
three

Please don't go I'm

scared I don't know

what's happening

squeeze my hand

hard as you can okay

can you do that

**love you so much
I didn't want you to
see me like this**

not going anywhere i'm

here i'm not gonna go

anywhere at all I promise

+ 1 MONTH   51

        this isn't you you're

        just sick you're sick

        it's like a broken leg

                          That's it.

                          Three.

          That's it you're nearly there.

              i don't want to be here

you can't do that or you'll break all our hearts

                        Breathe.

BRIGID   that's it

    Breathe

      okay that's good
    Out through the

            You're okay. You're okay.

                    You're okay.
                        he's not getting better

Hold my hand

            You're doing so good.

Four

            You're okay.
              Shh.

Brigid

You're okay.

five

I'm sorry I don't know
what's wrong
with me

Niall

I'm so sorry

I'm sorry

Brigid

You're okay.

You're okay.

+ 1 month, 1 day

The early hours of the morning.

They both look exhausted.

Pause.

NIALL	I didn't mean to scare you.
	BRIGID *shrugs*.
BRIGID	Is that what it's like? Every time?
NIALL	Not every time.
BRIGID	You've been taking your – ?
NIALL	Yes.
BRIGID	What did they say about the counsellor? How long is the list?
NIALL	Eight to twelve months.
BRIGID	Well, I don't think we can wait any longer, so we're gonna find someone ourselves.
	Because last night.
	You can't be doing that.
NIALL	–
	I don't think I have the money for a counsellor.
BRIGID	I'll work something out.
NIALL	Do you have the money for that?

BRIGID	I'll work something out.
NIALL	I'm supposed to move out next week.
BRIGID	I mean.
	What if I hadn't been here? What if that happened and I wasn't there? What then?
	You're staying.
NIALL	Some people don't get better.
	They just get sick one day and then that's them their whole life. That's you done. You're fucked. Goodbye.
BRIGID	I don't know if that's true.
	But if it is, I don't think that you are one of those people.
	Pause.
NIALL	I might have a shower.
BRIGID	Sounds good.
NIALL	Um.
	Thank you.
	She nods. He goes.
	BRIGID*'s left alone.*

+ 2 months

Brigid's flat.

NIALL *and* BRIGID.

BRIGID *sitting*, NIALL *pacing*.

BRIGID	And Niall, what would you say were your greatest strengths?
NIALL	That's a great question, thank you for that. I would say my greatest strength is my reliability. And my um commitment to doing a good job. And I'm also very *patient*.
BRIGID	Yes you are.
NIALL	*And* – I think – most of all, I'm dedicated to making sure every customer has a really positive experience.
BRIGID	That's very impressive.
NIALL	Thank you.
BRIGID	Now, Niall, can I ask you, how would you handle a difficult situation. For example, maybe an irate customer being rude to you?
NIALL	In what way are they being rude to me?
BRIGID	They're raising their voice, possibly using bad language.
NIALL	If someone was rude to me like that?
	I'd go for them. Physically.

BRIGID	Very funny.
NIALL	Violently, you understand.
BRIGID	Are you actually gonna say that though?
NIALL	I'd take their coffee and I'd throw it at / them.
BRIGID	Niall.
NIALL	I'd be polite and calm with them, try and resolve the issue. If I could not resolve the issue, I would get my manager or supervisor. And I wouldn't get worked up, even if they were being an absolute fucking dickhead.
BRIGID	–
	You know not to say / the dickhead bit?
NIALL	I know not to say the dickhead bit.
BRIGID	Then I think you're good to go.
NIALL	Do you need any help with your work thing?
BRIGID	Do you know anything about zoning and public housing?
NIALL	No. But we're different kinds of clever, so it's fine.
	MICHAEL DORAN *appears at the door.*
MICHAEL DORAN	Hiya. Sorry, I'm a wee bit early. D'you mind if I just use your bathroom?
BRIGID	Sure.
MICHAEL DORAN	Hi Niall. How you doing big man?
NIALL	Hey –
MICHAEL DORAN	Michael Doran. You're / looking well.

NIALL	Michael Doran, right.
MICHAEL DORAN	Is this interview prep? I'm not here. Ignore me!

MICHAEL DORAN *goes off.*

NIALL *looks at* BRIGID *like 'Explain'.*

BRIGID	Michael's giving me a lift in. And we're gonna get breakfast.
NIALL	Oh.
BRIGID	–

What?

NIALL	Nothing.

–

Is he... gonna be around more often?

BRIGID	–

He might be.

NIALL	–

Why're you smiling?

BRIGID	I'm not smiling.
NIALL	Yes you are.
BRIGID	Shut up.

MICHAEL DORAN *comes back in.*

MICHAEL DORAN	Right. Sorry, your sister told me that you had a job interview today.

Hope it goes really well.

NIALL	Cheers mate.
BRIGID	Good luck today.

Don't be scared.

MICHAEL DORAN goes. As BRIGID *is leaving:*

NIALL Have fun.

BRIGID Shut up.

+ 4 months

The outside bit of a pub, under a heat lamp.

NIALL *and* MICHAEL DORAN.

MICHAEL DORAN*'s bought a round.*

NIALL	Thanks for getting these.
MICHAEL DORAN	No worries mate. Cheers.
	You can get the next round.
NIALL	Okay.
MICHAEL DORAN	Or if we don't stay for the next round, you can always just transfer me the money.
	–
	Joke.
NIALL	Oh right. Ha.
MICHAEL DORAN	Are you not really a big man for the pub?
NIALL	Not recently.
MICHAEL DORAN	Ah well, this is nice then.
	'Lads' night.'
NIALL	Sorry?
MICHAEL DORAN	(*Exactly the same way as before*.) 'Lads' night.'
NIALL	Hm?
MICHAEL DORAN	(*Exactly the same way as before*.) 'Lads ni– You're having me going.
NIALL	Sorry.

MICHAEL DORAN	No, it's great! I'm up for the craic.
	Love a joke.
	–
	You got a girl on the go at the moment?
NIALL	Uh. No. I don't.
MICHAEL DORAN	Ah really? Good-looking guy like you? Start going to the gym a bit. Haircut. Get one of those eh. Nice fleeces. You'd do alright.
	You on the apps?
NIALL	Not at the moment.
MICHAEL DORAN	Anyone at work?
NIALL	I've only just started.
MICHAEL DORAN	But it's a coffee shop right? You'll meet interesting people there!
	And that's what it's all about.
NIALL	What do you do again, Michael?
MICHAEL DORAN	I'm in out-of-home advertising.
NIALL	What is that?
MICHAEL DORAN	That would be billboards. Selling billboard space. Coordinating advertising strategies. Electronic billboards. That kind of thing.
	Listen, if you wanted, I could help you get set up.
NIALL	Set up?
MICHAEL DORAN	On a dating app.
	Before I met your sister, I was on the apps, and I was, you know like, I was doing alright.

NIALL	Cool.
MICHAEL DORAN	No, I don't mean. I wasn't like… I wasn't like 'a shagger', but I was doing alright you know?
	Like, I'm so glad I met your sister.
	And I'm completely happy and, you know. Content. With her.
NIALL	Well. Thank you.
	But I don't think I want to be dating at the moment.
MICHAEL DORAN	Why not?
NIALL	I –
	NIALL *laughs*.
MICHAEL DORAN	What's funny about it? You'd do well so you would.
NIALL	What would I even say on a date?
MICHAEL DORAN	Just be yourself.
NIALL	What? Just like a big fucking loser who tried to set himself on fire?
MICHAEL DORAN	I wouldn't mention that initially. Maybe don't mention it at all unless they ask about, you know… 'the hand'.
	–
	I could help you. We could do a photoshoot. It'd be fun.
NIALL	You could advertise me.
MICHAEL DORAN	Exactly! Advertising – that's all dating is!
	'Dating is advertising.' (That's not bad. I should write that down.)

NIALL	You could put me up on one of your billboards.
MICHAEL DORAN	Ha, have you got ten grand to hand?
NIALL	There might even be an app for people who set themselves on fire.
MICHAEL DORAN	See, why do you have to – ?
	You don't have to mention it all the time.
NIALL	Sorry.

NIALL *starts ripping up a beer mat.*

MICHAEL DORAN	It just makes people a little uncomfortable when you make jokes like that. And people don't know how to react to them.
NIALL	Yep.
MICHAEL DORAN	But it's nothing to be embarrassed about.

MICHAEL DORAN *watches him rip up the beer mat.*

Why are you doing that?

NIALL	I don't know.
MICHAEL DORAN	Could you stop?

NIALL *stops ripping up the beer mat.*

It's not that you can't talk about it. I just think that, day to day, it's probably not the best idea to go and just like tell random people that you once tried to set yourself on fire.

–

So you're seeing your um. Therapist now?

NIALL	Counsellor yeah. We don't have to talk about it.
MICHAEL DORAN	No, you wanted to.
	How's that?
NIALL	Good. Useful.
MICHAEL DORAN	Great. It was good of Brigid to sort that. You're lucky to have such a good sister.
	Till you can give her a bit of space. Get her life back.
NIALL	Right.
MICHAEL DORAN	–
	I think it's really important to your sister that we get on.
NIALL	Of course.
MICHAEL DORAN	She's great. And we like each other a lot.
	And the attraction isn't just physical.
	We also have really good conversations.
	About lots of topics.

+ 5 months

A phone call.

BRIGID *and* NIALL *on one end.*

On the other end, their MUM, *in her home in Lisburn.*

NIALL	Is there anything new?
MUM	Like what?
NIALL	I don't know. Just.
MUM	No.
BRIGID	–
	So things are quiet there then?
MUM	What was that, Brigid?
BRIGID	Things are quiet there then?
MUM	No more or less than usual.
NIALL	–
	Is Steven there?
MUM	He's out the back at the moment.
BRIGID	What's he doing?
MUM	He's sorting out the bottles.
BRIGID	What do you mean?
MUM	You know what I mean, Brigid. The bottles.
BRIGID	I don't know what you mean.

MUM	The bottles.
	The.
	The recycling.
BRIGID	Oh right.
NIALL	How is Steven?
MUM	Why, do you need him?
NIALL	No.
MUM	–
	Right then. I won't keep you.
BRIGID	We should probably head on.
MUM	Right you are.
NIALL	So yeah. Happy Mother's Day.
BRIGID	Happy Mother's Day.
MUM	Thank you. Yes.
BRIGID	Bye.
NIALL	Bye Mum.
	NIALL *hangs up*.
BRIGID	There. That's that.
	For another year.

+ 6 months

A small room in a house in Belfast.

NIALL is watching MICHAEL DORAN do stomach crunches on the floor.

MICHAEL DORAN	and this one – is called a bicycle crunch – because of what I'm doing with my legs right here, see? Like a bike. And it's actually more effective than a regular crunch because you feel it in your abs *and* your obliques.
NIALL	Yeah.
MICHAEL DORAN	You see? It's just – huh – and then – huh.
	And the best thing. Don't need any equipment. You can just get on the floor and – huh.
	BRIGID comes in carrying a box.
BRIGID	Okay I think this is everything.
MICHAEL DORAN	I was just showing Niall some exercises you can do at home even if you don't have a lot of space.
NIALL	And I didn't even ask him to.
	They all look at each other.
MICHAEL DORAN	I'm gonna go bring the car around.
	Niall.
	Take care of yourself big man. Looking forward to seeing you when you're all

	settled in. And I'll send you the link for the thing I was telling you about.
NIALL	Thanks Michael.
	He shakes NIALL*'s hand, kisses* BRIGID *on the cheek, leaves.*
BRIGID	What's the thing he's gonna send you?
NIALL	He wants me to do an online course on cryptocurrency.
BRIGID	He's just being weird because he wants you to like him.
NIALL	Oh really? I thought he was just like that.
BRIGID	But you like him?
NIALL	Yeah.
BRIGID	I like him.
NIALL	Look at you.
BRIGID	–
	And you're gonna be okay?
NIALL	Yep.
BRIGID	And you'd tell me if you weren't?
NIALL	I would.
BRIGID	And you'd call me?
NIALL	I would.
BRIGID	Even if it's in the middle of the night, or I'm at work. I don't care.
	You call me.
NIALL	I will.
BRIGID	You promise?
NIALL	Brigid.

BRIGID	Fine.
	It's gonna be weird without you.
NIALL	You'll have space to yourself.
	–
BRIGID	I love you so fuckin' much.
NIALL	Yeah.
	She goes to leave.
BRIGID	What's that?
NIALL	What?
	She goes past him, to the box beside him.
	She picks up a lighter. Flicks it.
BRIGID	Niall why do you have this?
NIALL	That's not –
BRIGID	Why do you have a lighter?
NIALL	I'm allowed to have –
BRIGID	Can you answer me?
NIALL	Don't go through my stuff.
BRIGID	Niall.
NIALL	That's not – you wouldn't be able to use that as / evidence because it's illegally obtained!
BRIGID	Why do you have this? Tell me right now why you have this!
NIALL	Fine!
	He takes out a pack of cigarettes and throws it to her.
BRIGID	You smoke now?

NIALL	Yep.
BRIGID	You know these literally give you cancer? / Are you completely fucking thick?
NIALL	Yeah I know that. Everyone knows that.
BRIGID	D'you know how bad smoking is for you?
NIALL	Well I used to set myself on fire so I think this is actually a big / step in the right direction.
BRIGID	Don't Joke About It!
NIALL	Alright!
	–
	Gonna miss this. Our chats.
	–
	Can I have my lighter back?
BRIGID	Obviously not.
	BRIGID *looks at him.*
NIALL	What?
BRIGID	Come here.
NIALL	What?
	She goes to grab his arm.
	He moves away.
	She tries again.
BRIGID	Let me see your arm for a second.
NIALL	Why?
BRIGID	Come here.
NIALL	No. Get away.

She grabs his arm and won't let go.

She tries to roll up his sleeve, he kind of swats her away, but she keeps going.

BRIGID: Come here.

Take this off! / Take it off!

NIALL: Brigid! Fuck off! Fucking / get off me!

BRIGID: Just show me!

NIALL: Let go of me!

They struggle and she manages to take off his jumper.

BRIGID: What is that?

He has burns on his wrist and forearms.

One of them looks nasty, infected.

What are these?

What are you – burning yourself?

NIALL *can't look at her.*

NIALL: I'd just. Flick a lighter. And then press it onto.

Calms me down.

Just sometimes though.

—

I'm really sorry.

They're both very still for a second.

BRIGID: And why do you do that?

NIALL: Feels good.

+ 1 year, 1 month

Late at night.

BRIGID *on the floor, on the phone.*

BRIGID   And what are you going to do when we hang up?

—

Yes. I think that's a good idea.

MICHAEL DORAN *comes to the doorway.*

And you've got ice in the freezer?

—

And just. Message me later. If you don't, I'll only end up calling you.

Okay. Bye.

She hangs up the phone.

She's exhausted.

Did you hear all of that?

MICHAEL DORAN   I got the gist of it.

What's he need the ice for?

BRIGID   It's like a self-harm thing.

You're supposed to hold an ice cube for as long as you can, until the impulse passes. It's sore, but it doesn't hurt you.

You hold the ice cube. The moment passes.

MICHAEL DORAN	That's clever.

Pause.

You know if he ever did do something, nobody would think it was your fault.

–

No one would think that you hadn't tried / everything like –

BRIGID	Yeah that's not really the point.
MICHAEL DORAN	Oh no yeah / of course.
BRIGID	That doesn't / even factor –
MICHAEL DORAN	Sorry no absolutely.

I don't know why I said that. I'm sorry.

BRIGID *opens a laptop and starts to work.*

What, you're working?

Do you need to do that now?

BRIGID	Thing is I actually do.

BRIGID *notices him looking at her.*

What?

MICHAEL DORAN	You're beautiful.
BRIGID	I'm tired.
MICHAEL DORAN	Yeah that too.

A person can be both.

He sits down on the floor with her.

She leans on him.

+ 1 year, 4 months

A nice restaurant.

BRIGID*'s just come from work and is mid-story.*

MICHAEL DORAN *nods along, a bit distracted.*

BRIGID	I told you about him – Mr McCrory – he took us for history and he was one of those people who'd just '*say things*'.
MICHAEL DORAN	Right –
BRIGID	He said, 'there will only be significant political progress in Northern Ireland when the older generations are dead'. He said that to us, and we're fifteen, sixteen. Which is kind of mad in itself but the point is I remember him saying it.
MICHAEL DORAN	Yeah.
BRIGID	And even then I thought 'that's not very nuanced' or whatever, but then now I actually have to *work* with some of these people. (And we're really not supposed to have opinions, so please don't tell anyone I said this.)
MICHAEL DORAN	Who would I tell?
BRIGID	You have to work with these people and you hear some of the things they say when they think no one's listening and you're like 'How far have we actually come?' Honestly if you heard how they

	talk – and all they seem to care about are their petty little sectarian passion projects.
	So yeah, you spend enough time with them and suddenly you just think Mr McCrory's idea doesn't sound too bad and 'well let them fucking hurry up and go if they're going'.
MICHAEL DORAN	–
	Yeah.
	Who's Mr McCrory sorry?
BRIGID	That was his name. The history teacher.
	Sorry, how did I get on to all of that? What was the question you asked me?
MICHAEL DORAN	Oh yeah, I just asked how work was.
BRIGID	Right. It was fine.
	–
	Thanks for letting me just –
	Are you alright? Are you annoyed because I was late?
MICHAEL DORAN	Hm?
	No. I'm fine.
BRIGID	Ah.
MICHAEL DORAN	What's that? Is that your eye thing?
BRIGID	It's doing it again.
MICHAEL DORAN	You should go to a doctor.
BRIGID	When? When would I do that?
	What are you looking at?
MICHAEL DORAN	Nothing.

BRIGID	Do you know her?
MICHAEL DORAN	Who?
BRIGID	The woman who served us.
MICHAEL DORAN	No.
BRIGID	You keep looking over at her.
	And you look sweaty.
MICHAEL DORAN	I'm gonna get some more drinks.
	He gestures to the waitress.
	Listen, can we – eh – talk?
BRIGID	I thought we were.
	What do you want to talk about?
MICHAEL DORAN	Okay.
	Um.
BRIGID	Michael are you / alright?
MICHAEL DORAN	I love you.
BRIGID	What's wrong?
MICHAEL DORAN	Nothing's wrong. I just need to –
	–
	Okay.
	–
	For the past two years – on and off – ha – you have made me so happy.
	No, you have.
	And I think we help each other to – grow – and become the best versions of ourselves.

+ 1 YEAR, 4 MONTHS 77

                    And honestly, sometimes I think the best part of me is… us. The bit of me that's us. I really do think that and I hope you think that too.

                    And I'd like for that to be the way it is. For a very long time.

BRIGID   Oh shit.

MICHAEL DORAN   So.

                    With that in mind…

                    He gestures to the waitress.

                    With that in mind / there's something –

BRIGID   Michael are you about to –

MICHAEL DORAN   Sorry, let me just – with that in mind –

BRIGID   Michael.

MICHAEL DORAN   – there's something I need to ask you.

BRIGID   I don't think you do.

MICHAEL DORAN   You don't know what I'm gonna / ask –

BRIGID   Michael. I think I do and you shouldn't.

MICHAEL DORAN   What?

BRIGID   Don't.

MICHAEL DORAN   –

                    But you don't know what / I was –

BRIGID   Michael.

                    This was a very nice idea. But maybe we should just go back to yours and talk about this. Alone.

                    MICHAEL DORAN *deflates completely.*

MICHAEL DORAN Oh right.

Of course. If that's what you…

–

Um.

Well in that case I better go talk to the waitress really quick because she's about to bring over a glass of champagne with an engagement ring in it.

Won't be a moment.

He leaves.

BRIGID *is left alone.*

He comes back with a bottle of champagne and a ring box.

Sorry about that. That's all fine. I've paid up and they actually hadn't opened the champagne yet, so we can just keep that.

BRIGID I'm sorry.

MICHAEL DORAN Don't be.

I get it. When you pop the question, there's always a chance the answer might be 'no thanks'.

BRIGID It's not a good time.

MICHAEL DORAN People have long engagements. We could have a three-, four-year engagement and then by the time we actually had to do the final – thing – we'd have been together five, / six years.

BRIGID Well as tempting as that sounds –

MICHAEL DORAN You're right. We don't need to –

Why isn't now a good time?

You don't need to answer that.

BRIGID	–
	Is that the ring?
MICHAEL DORAN	I can return it.
	I have the email receipt.
	–
	Can we go? The waitresses keep looking at me.

+ 1 year, 5 months

Brigid's flat.

BRIGID *and* MICHAEL DORAN.

A laptop is open and some streaming show is playing on it, but they're not paying any attention to it.

MICHAEL DORAN	And when was this?
BRIGID	Do you want to turn that off for a second?
MICHAEL DORAN	What?
BRIGID	D'you want to –
	He shuts the laptop.
MICHAEL DORAN	When was this?
BRIGID	When I was down in Dublin.
MICHAEL DORAN	For your work thing.
BRIGID	Yep.
MICHAEL DORAN	Right.
	And what was his name?
BRIGID	Joshua.
MICHAEL DORAN	(Fucking hell.)
	And this was – ?
BRIGID	Down in / Dublin.
MICHAEL DORAN	Right. Dublin. You said.
BRIGID	–
	It was just a really stupid thing. That I regretted basically as soon as it happened.

MICHAEL DORAN	–
	Is that it?
BRIGID	That's what I wanted to say.
MICHAEL DORAN	What's his second name?
BRIGID	Why?
MICHAEL DORAN	Joshua what? I want to find him online.
BRIGID	Why?
MICHAEL DORAN	I want to know what he looks like. I want to see this guy.
BRIGID	I don't think he's online.
MICHAEL DORAN	Everyone is online.
BRIGID	He really isn't anyone, he was just this guy at the conference –
MICHAEL DORAN	And yet you fucked him? You love me and he's nobody and yet you fucked this guy?
	What's his second name. Type it in. Joshua what?
BRIGID	–
	I don't know his second name. Why would I know his second name?
MICHAEL DORAN	OH I'M SORRY.
	I shouldn't have ASSUMED that you would know the guy you fucked's second name. That was presumptive of me.
BRIGID	I was upset at the time.
MICHAEL DORAN	Oh you were upset.
BRIGID	Everything going on.
	I feel like…

	I'm trying to do a hundred different things and I'm failing at every single one of them and then I try to talk to you about it –
MICHAEL DORAN	This is not my fault.
BRIGID	I didn't say it was.
MICHAEL DORAN	I'm sorry you're *upset* sometimes. I'm sorry work is hard and your brother is sad and the whole thing makes you upset.
BRIGID	Don't be cruel.
MICHAEL DORAN	But just because you're upset doesn't mean you can treat people whatever way you want.

                              I love you.

                              I FUCKING love you. And I tell you that all the time and I know that I tell you that all the time because I make a conscious effort to do it, because I told you that my dad never said that to any of us and that made us all really sad so I always make sure that you know that I love you.

                              –

                              I want to be able to trust you.

                              But I think we're gonna have to make some changes.

                              BRIGID's phone rings.

BRIGID	It's Niall.

                              –

                              I'll be five minutes. I just need to –

MICHAEL DORAN	We're talking about something important right now.
BRIGID	I know.
	But I need to take this. Five minutes.

She answers the phone as she goes.

Niall, are you alright?

Calm down.

And she leaves.

MICHAEL DORAN *sits.*

+ 1 year, 6 months

Brigid's flat.

Morning.

NIALL *has just got up and doesn't look great.*

MICHAEL DORAN *is in running gear and Nina Simone is playing.*

MICHAEL DORAN	Sleep well?
NIALL	Uh. Yeah thanks.
	Where's Brigid?
MICHAEL DORAN	At work.
	I was thinking you and me might go for a wee run this morning? How does that sound?
NIALL	I don't know –
MICHAEL DORAN	Why, you got stuff on today?
NIALL	Not really but –
MICHAEL DORAN	Put some trainers on. D'you want a water bottle? I got you a water bottle.
	He passes NIALL *a water bottle, a little aggressively.*
NIALL	Thank you.
MICHAEL DORAN	It'll be good for you. Get some exercise, get the muscles going, blood pumping.
NIALL	That's really nice of you Michael but I don't really want to go for a run.
	Is that Nina Simone?

MICHAEL DORAN	I've got a playlist that I listen to in the morning.
NIALL	Every morning?
MICHAEL DORAN	Pretty much.
NIALL	What's it called?
MICHAEL DORAN	Good Morning Playlist.
	NIALL *smirks*.
	What?
NIALL	Nothing.
MICHAEL DORAN	Is that silly?
NIALL	Nah mate, I was just –
MICHAEL DORAN	D'you think that's silly?
NIALL	No. No. It's a good name for a –
MICHAEL DORAN	You and Brigid both do that.
	Laugh at people.
	The wee smirk you do sometimes.
NIALL	You alright mate?
MICHAEL DORAN	Yeah mate I'm alright. You alright?
NIALL	I'm alright.
MICHAEL DORAN	Then hey we're both alright. Brigid said you might be moving back in.
NIALL	Uh. Yeah.
MICHAEL DORAN	Why's that?
NIALL	It's just been a bit rough recently. Brigid said I could stay with her again if I needed to.
MICHAEL DORAN	Why, did you try and set yourself on fire again?

NIALL	–
	No.
	Just. Bad thoughts.
MICHAEL DORAN	Bad thoughts?
	That's rough.
	Sorry to hear that mate.
	And d'you call Brigid whenever you have bad thoughts?
	You call her at work?
	She said sometimes you call her at work.
	I'm not having a go. Don't get me wrong. Call her when you need to call her absolutely.
	But did you know she's doing a big presentation today?
NIALL	No.
MICHAEL DORAN	It's kind of an important thing for her and she's been working on it for a while, so maybe don't call her today unless you absolutely have to. But if you have to, then do.
	NIALL *nods*.
	MICHAEL DORAN *turns off the playlist*.
	So that's what happened last night? You got upset and you called her?
NIALL	Pretty much.
MICHAEL DORAN	You still seeing the therapist?
NIALL	Counsellor. Yes.

MICHAEL DORAN	Good for you. Is that expensive?
NIALL	Yes.
MICHAEL DORAN	How d'you pay for that then?
NIALL	Brigid. Brigid's been paying for it.
MICHAEL DORAN	You don't pay for it?
NIALL	(*Hates this guy so much.*) I don't earn a lot of money.
MICHAEL DORAN	Oh fair enough. Good that you have someone who can pay for that then. 'Cause normally it's just: can't afford it, can't have it.
	You're lucky to have such a good big sister.
NIALL	Yep.
MICHAEL DORAN	Brigid and I talked about it and I'm moving in at the end of the month.
NIALL	Oh.
MICHAEL DORAN	Yeah.
NIALL	Good for you mate.
MICHAEL DORAN	–
	She's struggling at the moment. And she wouldn't ever tell you this, but I thought if I was you, I'd want to know.
	Thought maybe you'd want me to tell you.
	Because I don't think I'd want to put that much pressure on someone I loved.
	Pause.
	I'm not having a go.

NIALL	Right.
MICHAEL DORAN	I do get it.

> Not personally. But I've known people who've set themselves on fire.
>
> I tried to think of all the people I know or knew who did it or tried to do it and I could think of twelve people. Isn't that mad? In the office, people do marathons, raise money, in memory of all the people they know that have set themselves on fire. More all the time.
>
> But. Can you imagine if we just fixated on that all day?
>
> Nothing would get done.
>
> Anyway.
>
> Think we've probably talked this to death. You want to go for that run?
>
> Last chance.

+ 1 year, 8 months

A phone ringing.

BRIGID, *in her flat.*

She's clearly about to go out.

On the other end of the phone, JACKIE.

BRIGID	Hello?
JACKIE	Hi there, is this Brigid?
BRIGID	Yes. Sorry, who's this?
JACKIE	Hi Brigid. My name is Jackie, and I'm calling from the community mental health and fire team.
	I'm calling about your brother Niall, d'you have a wee moment?
BRIGID	(*Split second of absolute dread.*) Why? Has something happened?
JACKIE	No, nothing's happened. I'm trying to get hold of your brother, and he's put you down as a secondary contact.
BRIGID	You can't get through to him?
JACKIE	D'you know does he have a new phone number at all? Or if there's a better way of getting in touch with him?
BRIGID	No. That should be –
	He's been bad at answering his phone –

JACKIE	Probably nothing to worry about. I'm just gonna try him again. Thanks for your time.
BRIGID	Sorry wait, why do you need to speak to him?
JACKIE	I'm a counsellor, calling from the community mental health and fire team.
BRIGID	You're his counsellor?
JACKIE	Yes.
BRIGID	No.
	He already has a counsellor. Her name is – I don't know but I can look it up.
	It's like Julia or something.
JACKIE	Okay Brigid, I've got a note here saying Niall was given an initial assessment. And I've got another note saying that he was put on the waiting list for a counsellor.
BRIGID	Yeah, but that was like ages ago.
JACKIE	–
	Can I just check, d'you know how long ago the referral was? Or that initial assessment?
BRIGID	Like a year ago? A year and a bit?
JACKIE	–
	–
	Jesus fucking Christ.
	Sorry. Shouldn't have said that. Fuck's sake.
BRIGID	That's... okay.

JACKIE	It's a mess, Brigid. It's such a fucking mess.
	Sorry for swearing.
BRIGID	No I mean –
JACKIE	But d'you see? There's your wee brother, waiting a year and a bit for anyone to see him and who knows what's going through his head all the fucking while. And – honestly love – that's not the worst case I've heard. Far fucking from it, you know?
	Everyone's working all hours and… they're just slashing money from… Some of them don't even think it's real. They'll think it's fucking real when it's them or their kids setting themselves on… D'you want to guess how long my list is?
BRIGID	Is it – I don't know – is it long?
JACKIE	It's so fucking long.
	Every street in this country, someone's setting themselves on fire, or thinking about it. Every fucking street it seems like. Sorry again for the swearing. You don't mind do you?
BRIGID	That's alright.
JACKIE	But he's got his counsellor now?
BRIGID	Yeah he sees someone.
JACKIE	Aye well fucking great for him then. Fine for him, but what about someone who can't get one? Someone who can't afford it and can't wait a fucking year and a bit. A year and a bit. It's a joke. I'm raging now.

	Just to say, if I was your brother's counsellor, I wouldn't be saying any of this, but I've talked myself up into a rage now. An absolute rage.
BRIGID	That's okay.
JACKIE	Now, what I'm gonna do next is I'm gonna have a cup a tea, a cigarette, and then I'm gonna call the next person on the list. Because, love, the list is long.
	Anyway, you're alright?
BRIGID	Sorry?
	JACKIE *notices something*.
JACKIE	Oh hold on Brigid.
	Niall's calling me back now.
BRIGID	He's calling you now?
JACKIE	That's right. I'm gonna let you go so I can answer it.
	Have a wonderful day now Brigid.
	God bless you.
	Sorry. I shouldn't have said that either.
	Long day.
	Goodbye.
	JACKIE *hangs up*.
	MICHAEL DORAN *appears at the door*.
MICHAEL DORAN	Who was that?
BRIGID	–
	Just like a work thing.

MICHAEL DORAN –

> Okay.
>
> We should leave now or we'll be late.
>
> *He goes.*
>
> BRIGID *looks at her phone.*

+ 1 year, 11 months

Brigid's flat.

Late at night, BRIGID *is calling someone.*

She's still dressed up from a night out.

No answer.

BRIGID *dials again.*

MICHAEL DORAN *comes home, also dressed nice.*

BRIGID	Nothing.
	MICHAEL DORAN *nods, then leaves the room.*
	No answer.
	BRIGID *calls again.*
	MICHAEL DORAN *comes back in with a glass of water, looks at her.*
	Still nothing.
	It's been like three weeks since we talked and even then. So I went outside to call him –
MICHAEL DORAN	Oh that's what you were doing.
BRIGID	Right. And again, nothing. And I just kept getting these images of him... You know?
MICHAEL DORAN	I'm sure he's fine.
BRIGID	Did people notice when I left?
MICHAEL DORAN	Well. Yeah.

BRIGID	–
	Well. Sorry.
MICHAEL DORAN	–
	I'm sure he's fine.
BRIGID	He stopped seeing his counsellor. Is he still taking his medication? I don't know. He never calls any more.
MICHAEL DORAN	Isn't that good? He used to call you every day. Isn't this better?
	The phone rings out.
BRIGID	Nothing.
	She calls again.
MICHAEL DORAN	You're ringing him again?
BRIGID	You know what he's like.
MICHAEL DORAN	I do. Believe me. I do.
BRIGID	–
	What does that mean?
MICHAEL DORAN	This is.
	This is a trap. I'm not gonna –
BRIGID	No go on.
MICHAEL DORAN	Isn't this what he wants?
	The phone rings out.
BRIGID	I don't think my wee brother wants to be mentally ill.
MICHAEL DORAN	That's not what I'm saying.
BRIGID	What *are* you saying?
MICHAEL DORAN	I'm not saying anything. I am *asking*…
	Some people do this because they want to be looked after.

	So, I suppose what I'm asking is does he actually want to set himself on fire, or does he just want you to look after him?
BRIGID	Isn't that better? Isn't anything better than wanting to set / yourself on fire?
MICHAEL DORAN	Does he actually want to burn himself or is it just like a cry for help?
BRIGID	How is burning yourself *not* a cry for help?
MICHAEL DORAN	It's something is what it is.
	And stop calling him your 'wee brother', he's a grown man! It's weird!
BRIGID	Are you actually this annoyed because I left your mate's stupid party?
MICHAEL DORAN	People noticed!
	All night you were checking your phone, checking your phone, and Wally even asked me / what was up with you!
BRIGID	Oh god forbid WALLY be concerned by my absence!
MICHAEL DORAN	And when you ran off, I was the one who had to go back in and say sorry about that guys, Brigid's feeling a bit sick –
BRIGID	I'm not sick.
MICHAEL DORAN	– and she's had to run home –
BRIGID	I didn't ask you to lie.
MICHAEL DORAN	– and I could tell no one believed me.
BRIGID	I'm not surprised no one believed you. I'm not sick.
MICHAEL DORAN	Ha. Well.

BRIGID puts her phone down.

Are you not?

BRIGID   Am I not what Michael?

MICHAEL DORAN   Are you not sick?

We don't see each other for like two months because you have to look after your brother. Fine.

I think to myself, you know what, that's important and I support / you.

BRIGID   That's very noble of you. Are you the best guy in the world?

MICHAEL DORAN   And I don't *say anything*!

He moves out. Great. We can get on with things. Then he starts calling you every single night and we have to spend every waking moment talking about your brother. Then I say I want to spend the rest of my life with you and you say no thanks and I say that's fine and then you FUCK SOMEONE ELSE because you're 'sad' and 'stressed'? What is that? Still I let it go because I love you!

BRIGID   You just love saying that don't you? That I fucked someone else.

MICHAEL DORAN   Well, didn't you?

BRIGID   Never that I slept with someone else, or I cheated on you, it's always that I *fucked* them.

What does that tell us about you?

MICHAEL DORAN   Stop doing that. It's not like a symptom of a bigger 'thing'. I'm not 'men', I'm just me.

	I'm saying for the first time in two years we have some peace and you can't stand it.
	So I'm over here thinking, when is he gonna be right? Ever?
BRIGID	That's not how it works.
MICHAEL DORAN	Maybe it's not him.
	Maybe it's you. Maybe it's the both of you. I don't know any more.
	Pause.
	This could be your life. Forever.
	Looking after him. Worrying about him. Scared to answer the phone.
BRIGID	I think he will get better.
MICHAEL DORAN	But you don't know.
	You said you felt like you were drowning. You said that to me.
BRIGID	–
	I'm calling him again.
MICHAEL DORAN	I'm sure he's fine.
BRIGID	You keep saying that he's fine, but you don't know.
	And one time he wasn't.
	So.
	Pause.
MICHAEL DORAN	I'm trying to help you, Brigid.
BRIGID	I don't need your help, Michael.

MICHAEL DORAN	Yes you do.
	You don't think you do, but you do.
	–
	I told Niall to leave you alone for a while. Stop calling. Stop coming round.
	Someone had to.
BRIGID	–
	What did you say to him?
	Pause.
	BRIGID's *phone rings.*
MICHAEL DORAN	Is that him?
	Doesn't that just prove my point?
	It's fucking *him*, isn't it?
	Every time you come running and he fucking loves that.
	Don't answer it.
	Brigid.
	Don't.
	Brigid.
	BRIGID *answers the phone.*
BRIGID	Hi.
	No it's okay.
	I was just worried about you.
	Yeah I can talk now.
	One sec.
	(*To* MICHAEL DORAN.) You should go.

I don't like you.

I don't really ever want to speak to you again.

Back on the phone.

Okay I'm back.

MICHAEL DORAN *leaves*.

He slams the door behind him as hard as he possibly can.

Pause.

She reaches for the glass of water.

She picks up an ice cube and holds it.

One.

Two.

Three.

Four.

Five.

Drops it.

Yeah sorry can you say that again?

+ 2 years

NIALL *and* BRIGID.

A bench by the river.

NIALL *has a blue plastic bag.*

He takes out two Diet Cokes.

He gives one to BRIGID.

NIALL	How's work?
BRIGID	Fine.
NIALL	How's Michael Doran?
BRIGID	We've split up.
NIALL	–
	Oh.
	I didn't know that.
BRIGID	You didn't ask.
NIALL	That's fair.
	Should've asked.
	I'm sorry.
BRIGID	I'm not.
NIALL	–
	Damn. I loved that guy.
	BRIGID *smirks*.
BRIGID	I tried to call you a lot.

NIALL	Michael Doran kind of told me to –
BRIGID	I know that.
NIALL	And then, I guess. I was doing alright.
	I didn't need to –
BRIGID	What if I needed to talk to you?
	Did that ever occur to you?
NIALL	–
	Honestly. No.
	–
	Did you? Need me?
BRIGID	No.
NIALL	–
	We can talk now. Whatever you want to talk about. I can stay all day. I got nothing on. We can go swimming? We never went swimming. We can do that now. Whatever you want.
	–
	I'm sorry.
	And I hope you're okay.
BRIGID	Thanks.
	Sad for now. But, you know.
	How's the café?
NIALL	I got a new job.
BRIGID	Really?
NIALL	I'm doing – I'm a teaching assistant at the college.
BRIGID	You'd be good at that.

NIALL

Yeah well.

I'm patient.

–

Gotta be really fucking patient, 'cause kids don't know anything.

–

–

Did I make you unhappy?

Do I make you unhappy?

BRIGID

–

–

–

Yeah.

I mean yes.

Sometimes you do.

Yeah.

Sometimes you make me unhappy.

I don't think I'm generally unhappy, but sometimes. Yes.

Sometimes being there for you is exhausting and difficult and I'm really unhappy. And it feels unfair.

It's not really about whether or not the situation is fair. It just is. This is where we are so this is what we have to do.

–

–

–

But.

If I had to choose between being unhappy sometimes.

If I had to choose between doing all this and you not being here.

I'd choose this.

I'd choose you. I'd choose you every time.

Every single time.

Every every every every time.

I would choose you.

Acknowledgements

The writers of the 2020–2021 Royal Court Writers' Group, led by E.V. Crowe.

The cast of the 2022 reading of this play: Rachael Rooney, Ruth Carnegie, Olly Roy and Tobias Cornwell.

Rachel Taylor. Imogen Sarre.

Alistair McDowall. Dylan Frankland.

Amit Sharma, Daisy Heath, Iain Goosey and Indhu Rubasingham, as well as the entire team at Kiln Theatre.

The judges and sponsors of the 2024 Verity Bargate Award.

Emma Jordan.

Catherine Rees. Conor O'Donnell. Cormac McAlinden. Laura Dos Santos.

Abi Morris. Áine O'Sullivan. Bethany Gupwell. Chloe Stally-Gibson. Ellen Rey de Castro. Erik Delin. Julia Nimmo. Katie Richardson. Millie Foy. Zoë Hurwitz.

David Luff, Eve Allin, Max Elton and the entire team at Soho Theatre.

Maddie Hindes and Sarah Liisa Wilkinson at Nick Hern Books.

Jane Fallowfield – without whom this play wouldn't exist.

Pamela Cassells.

Ciar. Fionnuala. John. Sally.

Finally, Jacqueline 'Jackie' Magee – much missed.

www.nickhernbooks.co.uk

@nickhernbooks